Need to Know
Solvent Abuse

Sean Connolly

Heinemann
LIBRARY

www.heinemann.co.uk
visit our website to find out more information about **Heinemann Library** books.

To order:
☎ Phone 44 (0) 1865 888066
▤ Send a fax to 44 (0) 1865 314091
💻 Visit the Heinemann Bookshop at www.heinemann.co.uk to browse our catalogue and order online.

First published in Great Britain by Heinemann Library, Halley Court, Jordan Hill, Oxford OX2 8EJ,
a division of Reed Educational and Professional Publishing Ltd.
Heinemann is a registered trademark of Reed Educational & Professional Publishing Ltd.

Oxford Melbourne Auckland Johannesburg Blantyre Gaborone Ibadan Portsmouth NH (USA) Chicago

Designed by M2 Graphic Design
Originated by Ambassador Litho Ltd
Printed in China by South China Printers

ISBN 0431 097941

06 05 04 03 02
10 9 8 7 6 5 4 3 2 1

British Library Cataloguing in Publication Data
Connolly, Sean,
Solvent abuse. – (Need to know)
1. Solvent abuse – Juvenile literature
I. Title
362.2'99

Acknowledgements
The Publishers would like to thank the following for permission to reproduce photographs:
Bubbles pp8, 11 (bottom), 20, 25, 27, 36, Camera Press p19, Corbis pp4, 23, Corbis Stock Market pp10,
11 (top), 29, 32, 40, Gareth Boden pp45, 47, Getty Images p49, Imagebank p37, Images Colour Library
p16, Mary Evans Picture Library p17, National Inhalent Prevention Coalition p51, Photofusion p22, 35,
Popperfoto p33, Robert Harding Picture Library pp21, 30, Science Photo Library pp7, 38, 42, South
American Pictures p13, Tudor Photography pp6, 14.

Cover photograph reproduced with permission of Tudor Photography.

Every effort has been made to contact copyright holders of any material reproduced in this book.
Any omissions will be rectified in subsequent printings if notice is given to the publisher.

Contents

Any words appearing in the text in bold, **like this**, are explained in the Glossary.

Solvent abuse

Inside every house is a range of chemicals that can lead to serious health problems, **addiction** and even death. These chemicals are not illegal drugs like cocaine, heroin and LSD. Instead they are the essential ingredients in a wide variety of household goods, including paint thinner, marker pens, cleaning fluid, nail polish remover and even air fresheners. All of these substances contain **solvents** – chemicals that **evaporate** at room temperature and can be inhaled to achieve a 'high'.

Fatal attraction

Solvent abuse is the deliberate inhaling of a **volatile** (quickly evaporating) substance in order to achieve a sense of **euphoria** (a feeling of extreme happiness or joy). It is also known as **inhalant** abuse, volatile substance abuse, glue sniffing, sniffing and **huffing**. Affecting children as young as six years of age, it is one of the least reported forms of substance abuse. In the case of some older users – those, for example, in the 'rave scene' – the term 'laughing gas' is the nickname for one of their favourite inhaled gases. This gives us a clue as to how they view inhaling generally.

Solvent abuse is deadly serious. Sniffing volatile solvents, which include most inhalants, can cause severe damage to the brain and nervous system. By starving the body of oxygen or forcing the heart to beat more rapidly and erratically, inhalants can kill young sniffers. One of the most alarming features of these deaths is that they can occur the very first time a young person experiments with sniffing. Other drugs, such as heroin, kill – but usually they kill people who at least have some idea of what they are taking, and how much. A young sniffer has no guidelines in the way that a drinker has with a pint of beer or a smoker has with a cigarette.

The solvent 'high' is often better described as a 'low', as the user can appear drowsy and listless.

Tackling a monster

This book will show not only how serious a problem solvent abuse is, but also how difficult it is to control. Statistics prove that it affects communities all over the world, both in cities and in the countryside. Although people have tried to restrict the availability of the products that can be sniffed – and the range of these products increases every year – it is impossible to ban or change some of the worst offending chemicals. Instead, a worrying choice of 'sniffable' products lies not just on supermarket shelves but inside the kitchen cupboards of most households.

What are solvents?

Strictly speaking, **solvents** make up only part of the range of products that can be sniffed in order to achieve **intoxication**. The other two main categories are **nitrites** and **anaesthetics**. Like solvents, these other groups of chemical substances are **volatile** – they **evaporate** quickly at room temperature and can be inhaled. Some drugs workers prefer to use the term 'Volatile Substance Abuse (VSA)' to reflect this range. Informally, many people refer to the practice as 'glue sniffing' since some types of model-making glues give off fumes that young people have inhaled. Whatever the term, the effect is similar. After inhaling the substance, the person experiences a **euphoric** 'rush', then possibly **hallucinations** and then a return to a state that resembles an alcoholic **hangover**. Inhaling most types of chemical can lead to a range of serious health complications and even sudden death (see pages 28–29).

Solvents

Volatile solvents can be either gases, such as butane gas fumes, or liquids, such as petrol or paint thinner, that **vaporize** at room temperature. The number of common products that contain volatile solvents has increased greatly in the past 50 years. Besides petrol and paint thinner, products with volatile solvents include spray paint, paint and wax removers, hair spray, deodorants, air fresheners, cigarette lighter fuels and painkilling sprays. They are also present in the gases used to power whipped cream dispensers.

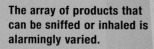

The array of products that can be sniffed or inhaled is alarmingly varied.

Nitrites

The term 'nitrites' describes a wide range of chemicals that relax some of the body's muscles. Some adults use nitrites to relax and to improve sexual pleasure. Often called 'poppers' or 'rush', some nitrite products are sold as room fresheners. Many come in capsules, which people break open. Whereas it is hard to replace the solvents used in many household products, many of the important nitrites – especially butyl and propyl – have been banned in many countries since the 1990s. As a result, this category has seen a decline in abuse since that time.

Anaesthetics

The main substance of abuse within anaesthetics is nitrous oxide. Doctors and dentists use this colourless, sweet-tasting gas for general **anaesthesia**. Nitrous oxide is called 'laughing gas' because it often induces a state of giggling and laughter. The real effects are far more serious. The gas can stop the flow of oxygen to parts of the body, including the brain. This loss of oxygen can lead to permanent damage to the nervous system and even death.

Amyl nitrate, one of the many body relaxants that can be abused, usually comes in small cylinders or capsules.

What are solvents?

How people take them

Solvent fumes may be directly inhaled from a container, plastic bag or saturated rag. People usually inhale through the mouth, with several deep breaths required to produce a 'high'. Some solvent abusers inhale to get the effects not of the product's primary ingredient but of its propellant gases, like those used in **aerosols** such as spray paint or hair spray. Spray paint also contains mind-changing solvents, which hold the paint particles in the spray.

What do they do?

Although there are many types of **volatile** substances that can be abused, the short-term effects are broadly similar. The inhaled fumes rapidly enter the bloodstream (and then the brain) through the lungs and speed up the heart rate. The first effects are confusion, slurred speech and dizziness, which can lead on to feelings of **euphoria**, a sense of unreality and even **hallucinations**. Sometimes a group of people inhaling together will have a shared hallucination. This first stage is usually followed by a brief period of recklessness, staggering, light-heartedness and agitation.

The effects wear off after 15–30 minutes leaving the user feeling drowsy and unable to concentrate. This **hangover** can last for up to a day, and may include headaches.

Some of these physical changes can be traced to a reduction in oxygen intake, others are the effects of the gases being inhaled. There is a reduction in heart rate and breathing, and most users experience dizziness, drowsiness and sometimes nausea. Repeated use or deep inhalation can cause confusion, loss of control and possibly loss of consciousness.

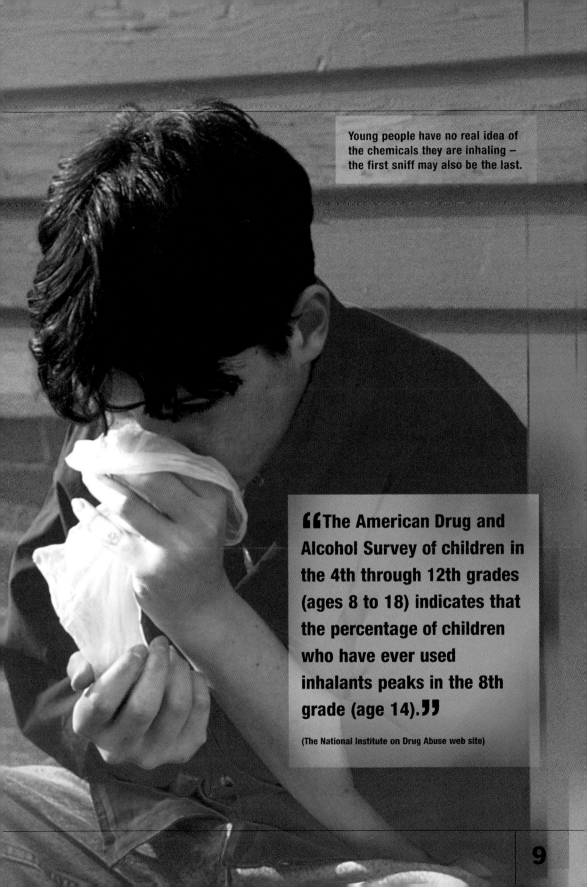

Young people have no real idea of the chemicals they are inhaling – the first sniff may also be the last.

"The American Drug and Alcohol Survey of children in the 4th through 12th grades (ages 8 to 18) indicates that the percentage of children who have ever used inhalants peaks in the 8th grade (age 14)."

(The National Institute on Drug Abuse web site)

A growing problem

Evidence suggests that **solvent** abuse is widespread around the world, and it is increasing. Most of the detailed studies have been conducted in developed countries – especially the USA and Canada. Other studies and even informal observation elsewhere help build a fuller picture of the problem. The UK, for example, is the only country to compile statistics of the numbers of deaths relating to solvent abuse – averaging two per week in 2000.

Monitoring the Future

The National Institute on Drug Abuse (NIDA) has compiled some of the most comprehensive statistics on the scope and trends in solvent abuse in the USA. NIDA's 1999 'Monitoring the Future' study, a national survey of 8th, 10th and 12th grade students (aged 14, 16 and 18), found that about 17 per cent of adolescents in the USA say that they have sniffed **inhalants** at least once in their lives. These inhalants usually include **volatile** solvents such as spray paint, glue or cigarette lighter fluid.

Using similar data from previous Monitoring the Future studies (which go back to 1975), NIDA has drawn some broader conclusions beyond the 'snapshot' that a one-off study provides. Using these figures, NIDA conclude that 15–20 per cent of those surveyed had inhaled solvents at some point, with 5–10 per cent of 18-year-olds using solvents during the previous year. The results from a number of other surveys suggest that among children under 18, solvents come fourth among the most commonly abused substances – after cannabis, alcohol and cigarettes. This evidence also suggests that the number of young people inhaling solvents is rising worldwide.

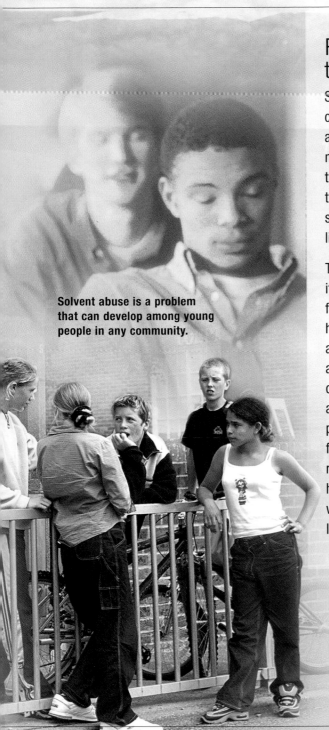

Solvent abuse is a problem that can develop among young people in any community.

Reading between the lines

Statistics, no matter how comprehensive, cannot tell the full story, and at times they can even be misleading. For example, the Monitoring the Future studies underestimate the true scope of solvent abuse because school dropouts, who tend to be more likely to 'sniff', are not included.

The very nature of solvent abuse, with its wide range of chemicals, presents further problems in trying to judge just how widespread the problem is. Solvent abuse often increases and then falls away in any area. Short-term outbreaks develop in a particular school or region as a specific inhalant product becomes popular in a fashion typical of teenage fads. Such a 'surge' in use can be reflected in survey results. When this happens, the study indicates a peak of what is in fact a continually fluctuating level of abuse.

A growing problem

One of the gravest omissions in studies of **solvent** abuse is any real indication of how many young people are abusing solvents in Third World countries – particularly among the poorest and often homeless people of the inner cities. Local drug-awareness groups and international charities must base their conclusions on observation and **anecdotal** evidence. Whether it is in Mexico City, Lagos or Manila, the evidence points to widespread and rising use. Many regular solvent abusers in these cities are younger than ten years old.

Explaining the increase

One possible reason for the increased use of **volatile** solvents is that more girls are joining boys in sniffing. Recent studies in New York state and Texas in the USA report that males are using solvents at only slightly higher rates than females are. Among Native Americans, who have high solvent abuse rates, lifetime rates for males and females were nearly identical, according to 1991 NIDA data.

Patterns of solvent use are similar to those of other types of substances. There are experimenters, occasional users and long-term solvent abusers. Canadian studies – typical of other developed countries – indicate that experimentation is widespread in all types of community. However, long-term use tends to be most common in inner-city areas and remote communities. These are places linked with unemployment, poverty, substance abuse and **dysfunctional** families. As in the USA, the Canadian studies noted that solvent abuse is common in some remote communities and virtually absent in others. Dependence, illness and death are linked with frequency of use. However, the 'Sudden Sniffing Death **Syndrome**' (see pages 28–29), which is the most common cause of death in **inhalant** abuse, can occur in first-time users.

❝The rates of solvent use for males and females have been converging over the past 20 years.❞

(Dr Fred Beauvais, a psychologist researcher at the Tri-Ethnic Center for Prevention Research at Colorado State University, USA)

Rates of solvent abuse are high amoung the young in Latin American cities.

A dangerous shopping list

The obvious reason why **solvent** abuse is so widespread lies in how easy it is to get hold of the products that can be sniffed or inhaled. The average household has more than 30 such products, nearly all of which are familiar goods. Many of these are seemingly innocent, so they are stored in easily accessible ground-level cupboards or shelves – ideal for young experimenters. Although some of the substances that are abused by inhaling – mainly **anaesthetics** and some gases – are bought and sold within drug-using circles, most solvent abuse is linked to the everyday items that most of us have around our homes.

The panel on the opposite page indicates the dangerous chemicals (many of them potentially deadly) that are found in a range of common household goods. People should be aware that it is vitally important to ensure that all of these are kept either well out of reach, or locked away in safe places.

It is a sobering fact that a supermarket checkout can often be an 'assembly line' of highly dangerous solvents.

Everyday items (by group) that can be abused

Solvents

Nail polish remover
Paint remover
Paint thinner
Correction fluid
Camping gas
Cigarette lighter fuel
Fire extinguisher
Spot remover
Degreaser
Paint spray
Hair spray

Nitrites

Whipped cream (canned)
Room freshener
Painkilling spray
Asthma spray
Spray deodorant

Anaesthetics

Liquid throat anaesthetic
Local anaesthetic

History

The notion of inhaling substances in order to become **intoxicated**, or 'high', is nothing new. There are indications that the practice goes back several thousand years. As with the earliest recorded uses of alcohol and cannabis, this practice had a spiritual and even religious dimension. Tribal cultures such as those in the Amazon region, even today, believe that individuals can only understand certain religious truths by achieving a trance-like state. They often reach this state by inhaling special mixtures of burning plants.

A dramatic natural setting added to the mystique surrounding the Oracle at Delphi. Greece lies in a volcanic zone, and mind-altering vapours might have seeped upwards through gaps in the rocks.

The oracle speaks

Looking back with the advantage of modern medical awareness, we can see how such inhalation probably played a major part as tribal cultures developed in the earliest civilizations. 'Sacred vapours' were recorded as part of the religious cults of the Assyrians, Babylonians and Egyptians.

Some historians also believe that similar vapours might explain some of the mystery surrounding the Oracle at Delphi, whose pronouncements were taken as sacred word. The pythia, or priestess of the god Apollo, would sit over a gap in the rocks and then go into a frenzied trance, during which she delivered the messages. This behaviour closely matches that of a **solvent** abuse 'high', and it is also reported that goats grazing near the same gap would behave oddly and bleat in an unusual manner. The conclusion is that some sort of volcanic gas seeped through the crack in the rock, providing the fuel for these trances.

Chemical advances

Inhaling fumes or vapours continued to be practised, although not widely publicized, for centuries after the ancient Greeks. Seigneur Michel de Montaigne, a celebrated 16th-century French essayist, recommended that surgeons use vapours more widely because they put patients in a 'proper mood for contemplation'.

The biggest change, however, came in the late 18th and early 19th centuries when nitrous oxide, or 'laughing gas', was first developed. Although seen as primarily a surgical aid, nitrous oxide gained popularity as a **genteel** way of becoming intoxicated. Famous people, including the poet Samuel Taylor Coleridge and the industrialist Josiah Wedgwood, attended fashionable nitrous oxide parties in England. At the same time, public demonstrations in Europe and North America displayed the effectiveness of the drug as an **anaesthetic**.

Ether and chloroform were developed as **anaesthetics** in the mid-1800s and, as had been the case with nitrous oxide, people also began to try them for entertainment. The Danish writer Hans Christian Andersen described such experimental sessions during a visit to Scotland in 1847. Although he noted the potential of ether as a painkiller during medical operations, he was critical of its social uses: in particular he scorned the 'lifeless eyes of the ladies' who had experimented with the drug.

The modern era

By the 20th century, advances in medical chemistry meant that other drugs largely replaced anaesthetics for use in surgery. Also, stricter laws controlling medical drugs meant that it was harder for the public to get hold of these substances. For roughly the first half of the century there was no widescale use of **inhalants**, but that position changed dramatically after the Second World War.

Starting within the USA and then spreading throughout Europe, Australia and beyond, people began to have more spending power and a rash of new household products flooded the market. Many of these products contained **solvents**, but the first widespread 'sniffing' came from a product that had been around for many years – petrol. Reports of petrol sniffing in the USA during the 1950s were followed by similar reports in India, Australia, the UK and elsewhere. It was obvious that there was a 'kick' to be had.

Punk music fans in the 1970s aimed to shock society with their outrageous actions that sometimes included inhaling solvents (glue sniffing).

The problem widens

Most of those who sniffed petrol were children experimenting with what came to hand. When parents, hearing of this new practice, hid petrol supplies more securely, these experimenters began a process that continues to this day – trying different household products to look for a 'buzz'. Glues and other solvents became commonly inhaled in the 1960s; by the mid-1960s every state in the USA had recorded such use. From then on a **disjointed** 'underground' spread word of various products that could be sniffed; at one point certain varieties of suede cleaner were popular.

The reputation of being 'uncool' limited the use of inhalants among teens until some punk music fans used them in the 1970s. A later generation of ravers in the 1990s turned to some inhalants, such as the liquid **nitrite** GHB (gamma hydroxybutyrate), as alternatives to ecstasy and other 'dance drugs'. Inhalant abuse remains a common and dangerous problem in nearly every country and especially among poor populations – both in cities and in the countryside.

Who takes solvents?

Solvent abuse is mainly a problem of the young. Very few adults sniff or inhale chemicals, apart from a few exceptions (see 'Alternative ecstasy', on page 22). It is a problem that crosses all sorts of boundaries – geographical, educational and social. Cases of serious solvent abuse have been reported as far afield as northern Canada and Alaska, the Australian Outback, the Scottish Highlands and the inner-city **ghettos** of Latin America.

Early experiments

Most people start sniffing solvents or **aerosols** 'just to see what it's like'. Nobody ever expects to come to harm, or to have a problem. Some people get into sniffing regularly because they like the buzz. They don't think of it as 'a problem', it's just something they do. Children as young as six or eight experiment by sniffing household products, often turning away from the practice after one or two goes. Others, however, continue to sniff, often because they believe that it makes them feel better during the difficult period of transition in their early teenage years. The peak age of **inhalant** abuse is fourteen to fifteen years: the abuse has usually dropped off between the ages of seventeen and nineteen.

Young people often have their first experience of sniffing in the familiar setting of a garden shed.

Masking the problem

One of the difficulties in dealing with the problem of solvent abuse is the nature of the drug itself. Public health officials and drug-awareness counsellors can usually get a reasonably clear picture of how many young people are taking some drugs. This is because people tend to respond honestly to questions in **confidential** surveys about drugs such as ecstacy and cannabis. Solvents, though, are different. For the most part, young people – even those who take them – do not consider solvents 'cool'. Even in the secrecy of a confidential survey a young person might not tell the truth about their problem.

Alternative ecstasy

While, overall most **solvent** abusers are the young (and very young) there are 'pockets' of users among older teenagers and young adults. Most of these people shun actual solvents and prefer to inhale gases – either **anaesthetics** or muscle relaxants – that are produced for medical or surgical purposes.

Many people who are drawn into the drug-taking element of the 'rave' scene, or dance culture, take ecstasy, LSD or amphetamine sulphate ('speed') either to heighten the dance experience or to stay awake for hours on end. Each of these drugs, however, produces known risks, so some dancers turn to what they wrongly think are 'safer' substances that can be inhaled. One of the most commonly used is gamma hydroxybutyrate (GHB). This was originally developed as an anaesthetic but withdrawn because of unwanted side effects. Moderate doses of GHB (which many people take in its liquid form) produce an effect like alcoholic

intoxication. People experience a lessening of **inhibitions** and a sense of good cheer, but it is easy to take too much. Taking too much GHB leads to a state of sedation, which can easily result in passing out and even drifting into a coma.

Other **inhalants** preferred by older users – again, with a concentration in the 'rave' scene – include the gas nitrous oxide and a range of inhalants known as 'poppers'. Most poppers belong to a group of chemicals known as alkyl **nitrites**. They have the reputation for enhancing sensations, giving a concentrated burst of energy for several minutes. A single dose used to come in a glass capsule, which was broken open ('popped') and inhaled. They are now packaged in small bottles.

Raves have often been linked to drug taking. Some dancers use the anaesthetic GHB, thinking that it is somehow safer than ecstasy or LSD.

Street children

Solvent abuse is not confined to young people in the developed world. It is common among the estimated 100 million 'street children' in the cities of Latin America, Africa and Asia. These are children who live by their wits, and they inhale in order to get to sleep, to lessen pain or simply to find a brief escape from their difficult and often violent lives. They choose solvents because many of them are ready-to-hand, often discarded as rubbish. Street children in Uganda inhale the fumes of aircraft fuel and petrol, and one study suggests that nine out of ten street children in Guatemala are **dependent** on paint thinner or glue. Wherever they may be, these children run all of the risks of any solvent abuser, but because of the poverty and violence of their environment they expose themselves to additional dangers each day.

❝Doctors and emergency room staffs need to be aware that the profile of the teenager who inhales volatile solvents is not limited to the ethnic lower socioeconomic classes.❞

(Dr C. W. Sharp, NIDA)

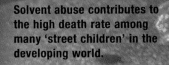

Solvent abuse contributes to the high death rate among many 'street children' in the developing world.

Getting hold of solvents

Most mind-altering drugs are illegal, so people can only get hold of them by breaking the law. This is true of cannabis, LSD, heroin and ecstasy, as well as dozens of other illegal substances. Even alcohol and tobacco – both legal nearly everywhere in the world – are removed from the normal 'market' because of age restrictions on buying and consuming them. These systems, one operating outside the law and the other within it, make it harder to obtain substances.

Solvents and their related **inhalants** are different. Apart from a few illegally inhaled **anaesthetics** such as nitrous oxide, they are essential ingredients in a range of products that have no real connection with altering the mind. Solvents are cheap and can be purchased legally in retail stores in a variety of seemingly harmless products.

It is possible to print warnings (about the dangers of inhaling) on the labels of some products. However, it would be unworkable to limit the sale of, for example, all paint thinners, glues, nail varnish removers and **aerosols**. Moreover, some drug officials believe that such labelling might backfire, simply alerting potential sniffers about which products might be worth trying.

Other avenues

This information relates to the diverse range of solvents that make up the bulk of the overall problem of abuse. As outlined in pages 20–21, most of these abusers are young teenagers. Usually these people stop using solvents between the age of seventeen and nineteen, but some people use inhalants past that age and into adulthood.

Teenagers and young adults can buy nitrous oxide **illicitly** at outdoor events, such as rock concerts, and on the street. This is where inhalant abuse begins to resemble other forms of drug abuse. 'Pushers' approach young people, offering them a chance for a 'quick high' in exchange for money. The nitrous oxide is often sold in large balloons from which the gas is released and inhaled for its mind-altering effects. GHB is sold as a powder, in capsules or most commonly in 30 ml bottles, which hold about three doses. 'Poppers' are sold in bottles that can be opened and inhaled.

It is all too easy for an unwary young person to get hold of dangerous solvents – a household cupboard can offer a choice.

Are solvents addictive?

Although the terms addictive and **addict** are often used in relation to drugs, most medical professionals prefer the terms **dependent** and dependent user. Part of the reason for this slight change of terms has to do with social matters: the word 'addictive' carries a sense of being uncontrollable and even unforgivable. 'Dependent', on the other hand, suggests a type of behaviour that can be overcome. Professionals also find it useful to talk of someone being either physically dependent or psychologically dependent on a drug.

A drug is said to cause physical dependence if the user continually needs to increase the dose to maintain the effects of the drug – a pattern called **tolerance** – and then suffers **withdrawal** symptoms when it is stopped. Alcohol (with its **delerium tremens**, or DTs) and heroin (with its cold turkey) are good examples of drugs that cause physical dependence. Psychological dependence, as the name suggests, is to do with the mind's 'need' for the drug to cope with stress or difficult situations. Alcohol also produces a psychological dependence, as do cocaine and amphetamines.

Difficult to assess

With **solvent** abuse, it is much harder to judge the extent of dependence since there are so many factors that confuse the issue. The main problem, of course, is with the range of substances that are inhaled. Although the results are similar (in terms of the 'high'), the active ingredient differs from product to product. This makes it hard to pinpoint a single chemical or drug – as one might do with cocaine, heroin, alcohol or even with active ingredients such as nicotine (in tobacco) and THC (in cannabis). Moreover, users tend to inhale whatever is to hand, or easily bought, and then move on to other substances that arrive on the scene or in the cupboard. Many users do show tell-tale signs of physical dependence, particularly the withdrawal symptoms of irritability and tiredness.

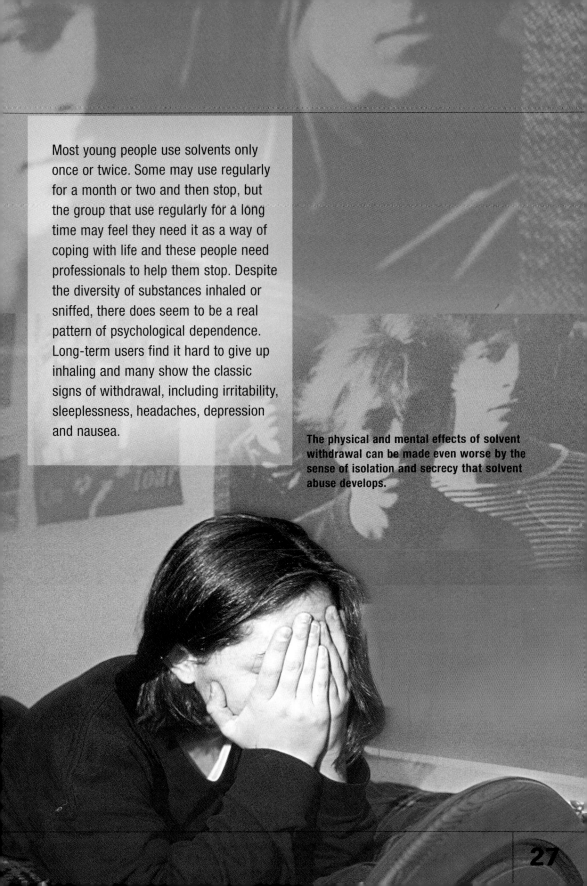

Most young people use solvents only once or twice. Some may use regularly for a month or two and then stop, but the group that use regularly for a long time may feel they need it as a way of coping with life and these people need professionals to help them stop. Despite the diversity of substances inhaled or sniffed, there does seem to be a real pattern of psychological dependence. Long-term users find it hard to give up inhaling and many show the classic signs of withdrawal, including irritability, sleeplessness, headaches, depression and nausea.

The physical and mental effects of solvent withdrawal can be made even worse by the sense of isolation and secrecy that solvent abuse develops.

A sniff of death

Solvent abuse leads to a wide range of negative problems, ranging from changes in behaviour and attitude to serious long-term medical problems (see pages 40–44). However, the biggest single concern linked to solvents is their ability to kill – sometimes after only one go at sniffing. Some of the reasons for these deaths are chemical – when ingredients in the inhaled products adversely affect some of the body's essential organs. Others are linked to the fact that someone who is high on solvents often loses touch with reality, leading to accidents with disastrous consequences.

Chemical reactions

Solvents are not meant to be inhaled, and even those gases such as nitrous oxide and GHB are meant to be taken under the strict control of a medical professional. Solvents, in particular, can do serious and lasting damage to the body. Some inhaled products contain chemicals that irritate or even eat away at the lungs and other parts of the body. Many industrial solvents are carbon-based, like our bodies. Most of the products can easily burst into flame. Smoking or using matches or a lighter could easily lead to an accident. Sniffing glue out of a plastic bag can cause suffocation. If someone passes out, the bag can remain stuck to their face. If someone throws up while unconscious this could also lead to choking.

Many of the sudden deaths caused by solvent sniffing are due to inhaling butane gas – lighter fuel. The liquid gas cools tissues in the throat, which causes them to swell. If your throat swells up you can't breathe. Other **aerosols** contain particles of the product that is being sprayed – like deodorant, hairspray or furniture polish. If you spray these into your throat they will coat the inside of your lungs and cause suffocation. Someone wanting to sniff from an aerosol must filter these particles out before they can inhale the gas.

Sudden death

One of the most disturbing consequences of solvent abuse is a fatal complication known as **Sudden Sniffing Death Syndrome**. Death occurs suddenly after the user is startled during inhalation — usually after being discovered by an authority figure or as a result of a particularly strong **hallucination**. The hydrocarbons of **inhalants** sensitize the region around the heart to **adrenaline**, which in turn has been produced by the startle reflex. The massive surge of adrenaline overwhelms the heart, which simply stops beating. Doctors can find no cause of death. Such a sudden death can occur any time that solvents are abused — even the first, experimental time. In one study of death from solvent abuse, there was no history of previous solvent abuse in 22 per cent of the victims.

A sniffer often experiences a bewildering distortion of reality, making it hard to seek help if a crisis develops.

A sniff of death

When the familiar becomes unfamiliar

The location where someone sniffs can be a danger too. Busy roads, railways, building sites, canals and rivers become extremely dangerous when someone has been sniffing **solvents**. They could fall in a river and not remember how to swim. They might think there's plenty of time to cross the road when there is not. These problems are heightened when the person inhales alone, with no one there to help or find help in an emergency.

It is usually too late to revive someone who has fallen victim to Sudden Sniffing Death Syndrome.

Grim statistics

Dr James C. Garriot is the chief **toxicologist** in San Antonio and Bexar County, Texas, USA. From 1982 until 1988, he studied deaths linked to solvent use. The results are alarming and reveal the concentration of solvent-related deaths in young males in the county. Garriot's research showed that 21 out of 39 people who died were aged less than 20. The number of females who died was 5, compared to 34 males. The majority of the deaths were not a direct result of solvent abuse, but were related to it. In a 'high' state, the victims had put themselves in extremely vulnerable situations. Ten lives were taken in accidents, nine by **homicide** and eleven through suicide.

These statistics highlight the danger that people who escape direct physical harm from the solvents can still expose themselves to. A range of **volatile** solvents were involved in these deaths. This variety reflects the widespread availability of solvents in household products. Garriot reported that goods containing toluene were the most abused, including paint and **lacquer** in spray-form. Petrol, nitrous oxide and refrigerants also directly and indirectly caused deaths in the county.

ffThe truth is, none of us had any idea that by breathing aerosol cans through the sleeves of our sweaters and directly into our mouths we could freeze our lungs and die. I saw it as an easy way to get a high and as an escape from everyday problems.**JJ**

(Olivia, quoted in *Hansard* 25 October 1994)

The solvents industry

Usually when we speak of a 'drugs industry' we are referring to a national or international network of producers, **traffickers** and dealers who control the flow of the drug to the eventual user. Likewise, there are illegal labs where people with scientific training produce amphetamines, LSD or ecstasy. Then there are those individuals and groups who grow and sell their own cannabis. Other industries, notably tobacco and alcohol, operate within international law but are nevertheless responsible for the production and sale of goods that change the way people behave.

Solvents are different. The 'industry', without exception, has no intention of having its products used for sniffing or inhaling. In fact, it is important for the companies involved to have their products associated with their intended, harmless purposes – whether it is a floor polish, adhesive or hairspray. It does these companies no good to be linked, however wrongly, with contributing to the drug problem affecting young people.

Serious difficulties

How can companies and concerned groups work together to control solvent abuse? The answer, unfortunately, is not clear-cut. Some of the efforts so far have even backfired. Below we look at some of the possible ways forward as well as the drawbacks of many of these proposals.

The best way to cut down on any type of substance abuse is through prevention. However, this is hard to achieve. Limiting the availability of **inhalants** is difficult because they make up a large group of everyday products.

Also, abusers simply turn to other products if their favourites become harder to get hold of.

Adding a poisonous chemical to the product to prevent misuse is also ineffective. Too many products would require such a change and this would make these products cost much more. Warning labels on packages may backfire because they allow children to identify sniffable substances easily.

High-profile seizures of LSD, cocaine and cannabis help limit the spread of these drugs. Unfortunately, this sort of scene cannot be repeated with solvents.

The solvents industry

Tackling the problem

Not everyone believes that every step towards tackling the **solvents** problem is doomed to failure. Governments, companies and drug-awareness organizations have worked on several levels to provide a united front against solvent abuse. They are aware of all the concerns mentioned, but they believe that some sort of action is needed. While it is impossible to **reformulate** the dozens of potentially inhalable solvent products on supermarket shelves, some steps have been taken. For example, freon (one of the most dangerous sniffed chemicals) has now been replaced with butane or propane products in most **aerosols** in the USA and in other countries. Pressurized whipped cream containers have also been redesigned to provide an alternative to using nitrous oxide.

Tied in with these moves have been efforts to make the public more aware of the dangers of inhaling. The UK's Advisory Council on the Misuse of Drugs (ACMD) has long promoted a message that 'solvent abuse is too dangerous, don't do it.' Linked to this message, which is aimed at children, is a campaign to make packaging clearer for adults. Its 1995 report on **Volatile Substance Abuse** recommended adding a SACKI warning (Solvent Abuse Can Kill Instantly) to labels and packages of high-risk products. Industry has responded by adding these labels on a voluntary basis to many, but not all, of the products linked with solvent abuse.

The Consumer Products Safety Commission (CPSC) in the USA also works towards publicizing the risks. The CPSC is a powerful **interest group**, and over the years companies have had to respond to its charges of health risks in a range of everyday products. It offers a telephone hotline for people with queries about potentially risky (that is, common and inhalable) products. Its web site contains detailed information about solvents and current campaigns.

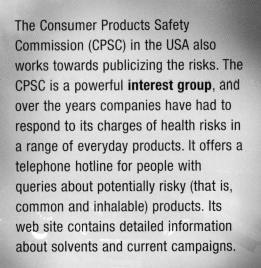

The large numbers of young people who gather at raves can make an easy target for those intent on selling drugs including a range of 'dance' solvents.

Family and friends

Although there are many reasons for becoming involved with **solvents** and 'sniffers' have a wide range of social backgrounds, this type of substance abuse is primarily a problem of the young. Legal drugs such as alcohol and tobacco, as well as some illegal ones such as cannabis and ecstasy, are used mainly by older people. As a result, children can learn about these substances from parents or older brothers and sisters. With solvents it is different – they are on their own, knowing little or nothing about what they are taking, what sort of 'high' it will produce or what sort of risks they are running.

Such ignorance is common among many first-time users of drugs, but with solvents the problem of ignorance continues as the young person experiments with a succession of new materials. Also, because 'sniffing' carries a social **stigma**, even with other young people, solvent abuse is often a solitary, secretive affair.

Drifting off

Apart from the many health risks associated with solvent abuse, there is a socially destructive side to the problem as well – and this is highlighted by the young age of most abusers. Any form of

Airing sensitive issues such as drug abuse is essential for any family. With solvent abuse older family members might even start out less well informed than younger ones.

substance abuse sends out shock waves through the family and among friends. The abuser distances himself or herself from other family members as well as from friends who are not abusers themselves. School work suffers because of lack of concentration. The abuser's **self-esteem** plummets, which in turn can cause the person to turn to drugs even more.

These 'typical' problems are magnified when the solvent abuse is taking place at a very young age. Children in their early teens (or younger) are at an age when they are forming the core of friends who might be expected to stand by them in later life. By removing themselves from the normal social events where such bonding takes place – in the playground, in clubs or on the sports field – young abusers have denied themselves the chance to form the sort of friendships that should help them. A 16-year-old who has begun to drink heavily or take drugs can often be steered back into normal life with the help of friends; a 10-year-old who inhales solvents regularly has no such lifeline.

Recognizing the signs

Because the problem is often hidden, parents should never simply assume that 'my child' would never become involved. Parents often remain ignorant of **solvent** use or do not educate their children until it is too late. Solvents are poisons and toxins and should be discussed in those terms. Unfortunately, parents and other family members are often unfamiliar with many of the tell-tale signs that a child is a **chronic** solvent abuser.

These signs include poor hygiene and grooming, frequent obvious episodes of **intoxication**, weight loss from decreased calorie intake and, most importantly, the conspicuous odour of the solvent. This smell is often present because much of the absorbed dose exits by the same route that it enters the body (via the lungs) so the odour can persist on the breath for many hours. A regular user often has red or runny eyes or nose as well as spots or sores around the mouth. The product may also be spilled during use, resulting in another source of the odour, as well as stains and flecks of paint or glitter on the face or clothes.

Finding products of abuse stored in unusual locations, such as a can of petrol under the child's bed or a large supply of a potential **inhalant**, often suggests inhalant abuse. Crucially, it is the child's behaviour that should be the ultimate warning. A regular inhaler will have slurred or disoriented speech as well as a drunk, dazed or dizzy appearance. He or she will also show signs of anxiety, excitability, irritability or restlessness.

Although this brain is healthy, brain scans can give conclusive proof of the damage caused by chronic solvent abuse.

How the family can help

Re-Solv (UK-based) and the National Inhalant Prevention **Coalition** in the USA have targeted parents as the best people to identify high-risk potential 'sniffers' and to pass on the stark basic information about solvents. Their fact sheets, web sites and regular bulletins help keep parents — and other concerned family members — aware of the severe dangers of solvent abuse.

❝I had some friends who tried to pressure me into this and on the other hand I had friends who respected me for being a strong willed person. Yes, I feel that since I didn't do drugs I've lost good friends. However, it is not my fault... they made the decision. They chose to leave me... and if they were a real friend they wouldn't have... ❞

(Anonymous contributor to The National Youth Anti-Drug Media Campaign kid's eye view web site)

Life with solvents

There is a huge price to pay for the brief and unpredictable high that sniffing **solvents** provides. The risk of death is always present, whether it is the first, fifteenth or hundredth time that someone has inhaled. Even those who avoid death, and continue to inhale, run all sorts of risks. These results range from poor performance at school and in social settings to a range of medical conditions, which, although not **fatal**, are often permanent.

Long-term consequences

Even within the relatively short period of peak solvent abuse (mainly the early teens) a number of longer-term effects can develop. Studies of solvent abuse have found evidence that **withdrawal** symptoms can occur (see pages 26–27) and that solvent abuse can lead to the abuse of other substances such as cannabis and cocaine. Prolonged abuse also affects the body itself, leading to damage of the central nervous system. This is a serious concern, since the effects of this damage – including **dementia** and brain injury – can be permanent. Poor performance at school is not simply the result of missing classes and losing sleep: the medical evidence suggests that brain damage leads to a loss of basic mental skills and co-ordination. The reason for this brain damage is, unfortunately, easy to trace. **Inhalants** are commonly designed to dissolve fats. So, because the brain contains a great deal of fatty cells, **chronic** solvent abuse dissolves these cells.

Chronic use of any solvent can lead to brain injury. There are, of course, many other long-term health risks related to specific chemicals found in some but not all products. The chart below outlines some of the problems linked with sniffing some common household products.

Dangers from sniffing household products

Product	Chemicals	Effects
Petrol	Benzene	Bone marrow disease, leukemia
Aerosol	Fluorocarbon, butane	Heart failure
Paint spray	Toluene	Hearing loss
Correction fluid	Chlorinated hydrocarbons	Liver and kidney damage
Glue	Hexane	Loss of muscle control
Paint thinner	Methylene chloride	Loss of oxygen in blood
Whipped cream	Nitrous oxide	Damage to the nervous system

This list is far from exhaustive, but it shows that solvent abuse leads to profound medical problems even if the user is lucky enough not to die from Sudden Sniffing Death **Syndrome**.

Moving on to other drugs

Inhalant abusers typically use other drugs as well. 'Children as young as 4th graders (10 years old) who begin to use **volatile solvents** will also start experimenting with other drugs, usually alcohol and marijuana,' says Dr Beauvais of Colorado State University, USA. He points out that adolescent solvent abusers are likely to use whatever drug is available, although they normally prefer solvents. However, older adolescents often look down on solvent abuse, which they consider unsophisticated – a 'kid' habit, he adds. It is not only children who are abusing inhalants. Current reports indicate that college-age and older adults are the primary abusers of butane (found in cigarette lighters) and nitrous oxide (laughing gas).

Solvent abuse is a problem in itself but it can also lead to involvement with hard drugs such as heroin and cocaine.

Airing the issues

Because many young people are solitary solvent abusers they never realize that their habit is part of a wider, international problem. Learning more about the experience of others who have abused solvents enables them to face up to their own problem; at the same time, it helps others who have done just that and want to become 'clean'.

The small Alaskan town of Bethel held its Third Annual Inhalant Abuse Conference in March 2000. Its theme was 'Taking Action… Using our Knowledge'. The knowledge in this case came from the personal stories of two local families. Sixteen-year-old Paula Albert and the family of Teresa Jimmie spoke about their experiences with inhalants on the first day of the conference. Paula said depression led her to abuse inhalants but with a friend's help she stopped **huffing**. As part of her recovery, Paula shares her stories with other young people. Teresa Jimmie died from huffing three years ago. Her family shared her story to prevent others from losing loved ones.

"Children from any social class may try sniffing. This does not necessarily mean their parents have failed or brought them up badly. It's more likely to be one of the 'disobedient' and sometimes risky things that youngsters do."

(Richard Ives, *Solvents: A Parents Guide*)

Legal matters

Lawyers run into many of the same problems faced by producers of **solvents**. It is unworkable – if not outright impossible – to make all solvents illegal for young people to buy. This has not worked well with tobacco and alcohol. Many people also argue that it would be misguided and wrong to make it illegal to sell such products: as so many of them have legitimate uses. On the other hand, many other people view this approach as an effective strategy. In their view, this practice makes the point that society condemns **inhalant** abuse. The British system adopts this strategy.

Interpreting the laws

Using this approach, the law in England and Wales makes it illegal for anyone to supply someone under the age of eighteen with substances that 'will be used to achieve **intoxication**'. This is aimed at retailers, to prevent the sale of solvents to those under eighteen. Nevertheless the law does not control the use of these substances to achieve intoxication. In other words, it is illegal to sell solvents to a young person, but the same person can use solvents to get high if they have somehow got hold of them.

Canada has no federal (national) law prohibiting the possession or use of solvents, but some Canadian provinces have been more specific. Alberta, for example, makes it an offence to use 'an intoxicating vapour to induce intoxication, **euphoria** or **hallucinations** and to assist or cause another person to inhale or otherwise introduce into his system such a vapour'.

The legal position in the USA is even less clear-cut. Solvents are not regulated under the Controlled Substances Act (CSA), a law that covers cocaine, cannabis and many other drugs. However, a few states place a restriction on the sale of these products to minors. There is a far more effective measure that does seem to work in dealing with these same solvent abusers who are school-age children. This approach, known as '**zero tolerance**', punishes those who use, sell or sometimes even possess solvent-abuse products, with immediate expulsion from school. The decentralized law-making system of the USA means that

Governments face a tough problem of limiting the sale of dangerous solvents without ruining the livelihood of shops and stores.

individual states, or sometimes individual school districts, have greater powers than those in other countries. This extra power means that they can apply zero-tolerance rules even if the national or state law is far less harsh or specific.

❝Students who sell, give, deliver, possess, use or are under the influence of drugs, alcoholic beverages or abusable chemicals must be expelled.❞

(Clear zero tolerance legislation from the 'Safe Schools Charter' in the US state of Texas)

Treatment and counselling

Most forms of substance abuse can be addressed and often overcome with a combination of short-term treatment and longer-term counselling. This approach can work even with those substances with the highest rates of **dependence** – such as heroin, tobacco and alcohol. Crucially, these treatments depend initially on the abuser coming forward and admitting the problem. **Solvent** abuse is different and in some ways more difficult to deal with. Most abusers simply will not admit to their use of solvents. The wide range of abused substances, with their diverse chemical compositions, makes it virtually impossible to decide on a clear-cut system of treatment. More importantly – and this is the problem with so many areas of solvent abuse – it is the extreme youth of the abusers that stands in the way of systematic courses of treatment.

Steering clear of danger

'Treatment' for solvent abuse often means minimizing the risks faced by the solvent abuser rather than actually getting them to stop. It often amounts to direct first aid for those who are suffering from one of the many complications arising from the practice. Again, it is often hard to identify what chemical is the culprit in a particular instance, but drug-awareness groups do offer guidance in dealing with a person who needs assistance (see page 48, 'Taking sensible action').

In addition to this advice, there are some vital bits of information that could save the life of someone who is intent on inhaling. Do not let them wander off on their own. The effects will hit them so quickly, they might not be able to handle them and feel scared and out of control. They must make sure that there is always someone with them who can fetch help if something goes wrong. Never ever let anyone spray **aerosols** directly down their throat. They are extremely cold and can freeze the throat, causing breathing to stop. If someone is a glue-sniffer, never let them put plastic bags over their head – it is easy to suffocate.

Teenagers should be aware of the warning signs of a solvent crisis. Quick thinking by friends can often save a victim's life.

Education and publicity

Treatment facilities for **solvent** abusers are rare and difficult to find. Users suffer a high rate of relapse, and require 30 – 40 days or more of **detoxification**. They suffer **withdrawal** symptoms, which can include **hallucinations**, nausea, excessive sweating, hand tremors, muscle cramps, headaches, chills and **delirium tremens**. Follow-up treatment is very important. Many of the drug-awareness organizations listed in this book (see pages 52–53) can provide details of the nearest treatment facility; they also provide telephone hotlines for advice on treatment.

Prevention, rather than treatment, is far more effective. Educators and drugs counsellors agree that this information must be presented clearly to children before the age when they might begin experimenting. Such educational systems have been particularly successful in Native American communities of the USA and Canada. Prevention workers are especially effective if they are from the local community and can help instil a sense of pride in shared cultural values.

Taking sensible action

Re-Solv, the UK-based organization that deals with solvent abuse, provides some basic first-aid advice for anyone who is with a person who is high on solvents and needs help:

1. Try to sit them upright, or if they are unconscious put them in the recovery position (if you know it). This involves laying the person on his or her side, loosening their clothing and ensuring that there is nothing too close by to make them feel hemmed in.
2. Reassure them. Tell them that they are going to be okay, and try to keep calm yourself – sudden shocks or movements might kill them.
3. Call an ambulance. Don't be scared to tell the ambulance people what's been taken: if they don't know what the problem is, they can't help.

Classroom visits by drug counsellors provide a chance for informal exchanges about solvents and other drugs.

National Inhalants & Poisons Awareness Week

In the USA, communities are fighting the abuse of solvents by becoming involved in National **Inhalants** and Poisons Awareness Week (NIPAW). This annual event, held in March, has been the idea of the National Inhalant Prevention **Coalition**. Increasing awareness through a community-based project informs young people about the dangers of solvent abuse. Also it allows them to come into contact with people who have experience of working with solvent abuse. NIPAW has an all-inclusive attitude to its campaign and involves a large cross-section of a community. Schools and youth groups are the main focus, but health organizations, police departments, the media and other groups are involved too. The Awareness Week is very popular. In 2001, 46 states took part and involved over 800 organizations.

People to talk to

Although **solvent** abuse has increased dramatically over the years, many young people – the very people most at risk – have no way of finding more information. Too often, they are solitary experimenters who have no contact with other users, let alone people who could provide the full picture. What they do learn is often distorted by rumour and hearsay, about excellent 'buzzes' or 'rushes', but with no mention of the potentially fatal side effects of sniffing even once. This type of **peer pressure** is not helpful, but it is a strong and persuasive force.

A two-way street

There are, however, people who can put things in a different perspective – either by giving first-hand accounts of their own drug experiences or by outlining the clear dangers of any drug abuse. Parents and older family members are usually the best people to turn to first. In some ways, it could be as important for the parents as it is for the children to have such a discussion, since many parents – even those who are aware of other drugs – ignore the risks of solvent abuse. The 1999 Partnership for a Drug-Free America Attitude Tracking Study showed that although most parents say they have talked to their children about drugs, only about half have spoken with their children specifically about solvent abuse. The same study found that parents often underestimate the use of **inhalants**, with only 20 per cent of parents believing it is extremely or very likely that their child could be using solvents.

Experienced advice

The UK has a wide range of telephone contacts, many of them toll-free and most of them anonymous, where young people can find out more about solvents and other drugs. Many of the organizations listed in the Information and advice section (pages 52–53) are specialist phone lines. They provide such a telephone service, or they can suggest local agencies. Others are geared specifically to queries coming from younger people. Whether you approach one of these organizations, or a family member, a youth leader or teacher, the important thing is to be able to talk – and listen – freely about your concerns. Sharing a problem or worry is the first step to solving it.

❝Parents must be constantly aware of their children's activities and behaviour, and pay attention to signs of inhalant use, such as missing household items, soaked rags, and chemical smells on clothing.❞

(Edward H. Jurith, Acting Director of the US Office of National Drug Control Policy)

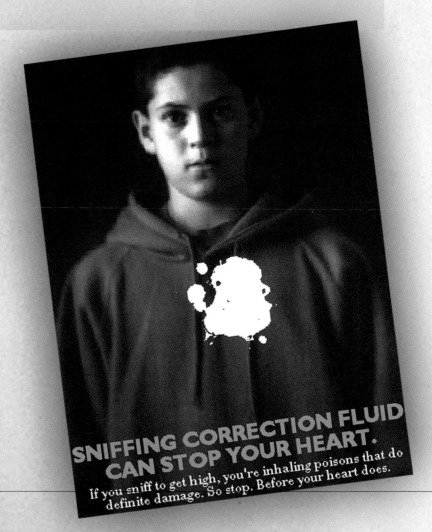

SNIFFING CORRECTION FLUID CAN STOP YOUR HEART.
If you sniff to get high, you're inhaling poisons that do definite damage. So stop. Before your heart does.

Information and advice

The UK is well served by organizations providing advice, counselling and other information relating to drug use. All of the contacts listed on these pages are helpful starting points for obtaining such advice or for providing confidential information over the telephone or by post.

Contacts in the UK

ADFAM, Tel: 0207 928 8900
This is a national UK hotline for the friends and families of drug users. It provides confidential support and information to anyone who is worried that someone close to them is using drugs.

British Association for Counselling (BAC)
1 Regent Place, Rugby CV21 2PJ
The BAC has an extensive directory of counselling services relating to drugs and other issues in the UK. Enquiries are by post. Enclose a SAE for a list of counsellors in your area.

Narcotics Anonymous
UK Service Office, PO Box 198J
London N19 3LS, Tel: 0207 730 0009
Narcotics Anonymous (NA) is a network of self-help groups tackling the problem of drug **dependence** on the same lines as those of Alcoholics Anonymous.

National Drugs Helpline
Tel: 0800 776600
The Helpline provides a toll-free telephone contact for all aspects of drug use and has a database covering all of the British Isles for further information about specific drugs or regional information.

Release, Tel: 0207 729 9904
Release operates a 24-hour helpline which provides advice on drug use and legal issues surrounding the subject.

Re-Solv
30A High Street, Stone, Staffordshire
ST15 8AW, Tel: 0808 800 2345
Re-Solv is Britain's leading organization concentrating on **solvent** abuse, providing general information and educational material about substance misuse.

Youth Access, 1A Taylors Yard
67 Alderbrook Road, London SW12 8AD
Tel: 0208 772 9900
Youth Access is an organization that refers young people to their local counselling service. It has a database of approximately 350 such services throughout the UK.

Contacts in the USA

Child Welfare League of America
440 First Street N.W., Washington,
DC 20001, Tel: (202) 638-2952
The Child Welfare League of America, based in Washington, provides useful contacts across the country, in most areas relating to young people's problems, many of them related to drug involvement.

DARE America
PO Box 775, Dumfries, VA 22026
Tel: (703) 860-3273
Drug Abuse Resistance and Education (DARE) America is a national organization that links law-enforcement and educational resources to provide up-to-date and comprehensive information about all aspects of drug use.

National Clearinghouse for Alcohol and Drug Information
1-800-729-6686

National Drug and Alcohol Treatment Referral Service
1-800-662-HELP

National Inhalant Prevention Coalition
1-800-269-4237
web site: www.inhalants.org

Youth Power
300 Lakeside Drive, Oakland, CA 94612
Tel: (510) 451-6666, ext. 24
Youth Power is a nationwide organization involved in widening awareness of drug-related problems. It sponsors clubs and local affiliates across the country in an effort to help young people make their own sensible choices about drugs, and to work against the negative effects of **peer pressure**.

Contacts in Australia

ACDA, PO Box 269, Woden, ACT 2606
web site: www.adca.org.au
The Alcohol and other Drugs Council of Australia (ADCA), based in the Capital Territory, gives an overview of drug-awareness organizations in Australia. Most of their work is carried out over the Internet but the postal address provides a useful link for those who are not online.

Australian Drug Foundation
409 King Street, West Melbourne,
VIC 3003, Tel: 03 9278 8100
The Australian Drug Foundation (ADF) has a wide range of information on all aspects of drugs, their effects and the legal position in Australia. It also provides handy links to both state and local based drug organizations.

Further reading

Buzzed, by Cynthia Kuhn, Scott Swartzwelder and Wilkie Wilson; New York and London: W.W. Norton and Company, 1998

Drugs, by Anita Naik; Part of Wise Guides Series; London: Hodder Children's Books, 1997

Drugs and the Party Line, by Kevin Williamson; London: Canongate Books Ltd, 2001

Drugs: The Facts, HEA leaflet; London: Health Education Authority, 1997

Drugs Wise, by Melanie McFadyean; Cambridge: Icon books, 1997

Solvents: A Parents Guide, by Richard Ives; London: Department of Health, 1992

Street Drugs, by Andrew Tyler; London: Coronet, 2nd edition, 1995

Taking Drugs Seriously, A Parent's Guide to Young People's Drug Use, by Julian Cohen and James Kay; London: Thorsons, 1994

The Score: Facts about Drugs, HEA leaflet; London: Health Education Authority, 1998

Glossary

addict
someone who is dependent on a substance

adrenaline
naturally produced hormone that increases heart rate and blood pressure as a result of stress or excitement

aerosol
product that emits its contents in the form of a fine spray

anaesthesia
lessening of the sensation of pain, usually during an operation. This can include producing a loss of conciousness.

anaesthetics
drugs or medicines that produce a state of anaesthesia (see above)

anecdotal
based on stories that have not been backed up with laboratory tests

coalition
group of like-minded individuals or organizations

chronic
continuing over a long period of time

confidential
usually, information that is private and not passed on to anyone else

delirium tremens
series of nightmare-like images and shaking that occurs when someone who is dependent on alcohol goes without it

dementia
severe damage to, or loss of, the ability to think clearly

dependent
needing a substance because of a physical or psychological craving

detoxification
getting rid of unwanted or damaging chemicals from the body

disjointed
separate, not unified

dysfunctional
not operating or behaving according to normal standards

euphoria
state of extreme happiness or joy

euphoric
experiencing a sense of extreme happiness or joy

evaporate
to go from liquid to gas form by being absorbed in the air

fatal
causing death

genteel
acceptable in 'polite society'

ghetto
run-down area of a city where people live because of their poverty

hallucination
waking dream where a person cannot distinguish between reality and sounds and images inside his or her head

hangover
feeling of being unwell that follows a period of intoxication

homicide
legal word for murder

huffing
slang term for inhaling solvents

illicitly
illegal

inhalant
something that is breathed in

inhibitions
thoughts that stop people from behaving in an extreme way

interest group
group that tries to influence government policy

intoxicated
having lost control of behaviour because of alcohol or drugs

lacquer
paint that gives a polished look to a surface

nitrite
one of the many drugs that relax certain muscles within the body

peer pressure
pressure to behave in a certain way, put on by peers, people of the same age or importance

reformulate
change the chemical make-up of something

self-esteem
ability to feel happy about yourself

solvent
liquid that can dissolve many other substances

stigma
something that is an embarrassment

syndrome
set of symptoms that occur together

tolerance
the need to take more and more of a drug in order to achieve the initial effects

toxicologist
someone who studies the effects of poisons on human beings

trafficker
someone who transports illegal drugs, usually over long distances or across international borders

vaporize
convert or be converted into vapour

volatile
evaporating rapidly into a vapour in the air

withdrawal
negative feelings (either physical or psychological) when an addict stops taking a particular substance

zero tolerance
disciplinary policy in schools that punishes even first-time drug offenders with immediate expulsion

Index

Titles in the *Need to Know* series include:

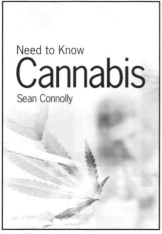

Need to Know
Cannabis
Sean Connolly

Hardback   0 431 09795 X

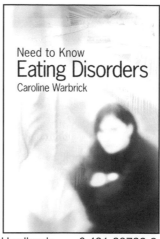

Need to Know
Eating Disorders
Caroline Warbrick

Hardback   0 431 09799 2

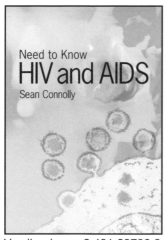

Need to Know
HIV and AIDS
Sean Connolly

Hardback   0 431 09796 8

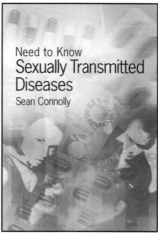

Need to Know
Sexually Transmitted Diseases
Sean Connolly

Hardback   0 431 09797 6

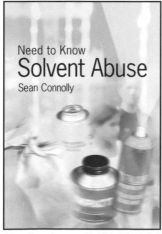

Need to Know
Solvent Abuse
Sean Connolly

Hardback   0 431 09794 1

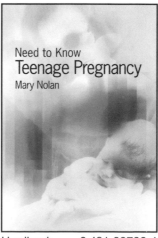

Need to Know
Teenage Pregnancy
Mary Nolan

Hardback   0 431 09798 4

Find out about the other titles in this series on our website www.heinemann.co.uk/library